A DELIGH

LILY FRO

This series includes the following titles:

PIGGY WIG'S HOME
LILY FROG'S HOME
MICKEY MOLE'S HOME
BONNY BUNNY'S HOME

Ramboro Books, 64 Pentonville Road, London N1
© Copyright

A NOT SO COSY DOZE

Lily Frog was having an afternoon nap. She had been up since early morning, baking for a party she was giving. Some time ago, a storm had begun, but Lily felt safe in her home in the lily pool near the big stream.

A bang woke Lily. The big stream had burst. It swooshed into her house and picked up everything it could carry, including the orange stool from under her feet and the pink rug from her legs; it even picked Lily up herself.

She could hear the walls of her little home creaking as she was carried off. Lily knew she would never see her little home again.

THE RESCUE

Swimming hard, so that the stream would not carry her away, Lily came up to the surface.

Already the storm had gone and the sun was coming out. Her big mixing bowl, the one in which she used to make all her party cakes, came floating up and she seized it. She did not want to lose that. Fay Fieldmouse had been coming to visit her and was asking if she should save a saucepan she had spotted. Lily called "yes" and Fay leapt in using a stick to paddle it to shore.

Then Daniel Duck flapped up and rescued the shopping basket that was Lily's favourite.

BRAVE LILY

All in all, Lily and her friends managed to save quite a few of her things. At the same time, Lily lost her skirt, but Fay noticed it caught up on a twig by the stream and went to fetch it.

Putting on a big smile, Lily climbed out of the water and put on her best pink hat, wet as it was. She was trying to tell her friends not to worry, things could be worse. Daniel, however, knew Lily was being brave for their sake. Things could not be much worse. Lily did not have a home and would never again feel safe in her old pool. Saying that he was going to find her some place to live, he paddled off.

PASSING ON THE NEWS

The growling of the stream had changed to a murmur as Daniel swam along close to the bank. It seemed to be saying that it was sorry for the trouble it had caused. He quacked that it should be sorry and Betty Butterfly and Benji Blue Tit heard him. They wanted to know what had happened. While Daniel told them, Slater Squirrel came along and listened. Betty, Benji and Slater were all upset for Lily. She had always been kind and helpful to everyone. They felt they should help her in their turn.

When Daniel paddled on, they discussed what they should do.

THE IDEA

Benji and Betty flew up to Slater's home in a tree and there talked for a long time. What they needed was a safe pool where Lily could live. They all agreed, but could not think of one.

Betty suggested asking Roberta Rabbit. Roberta ran a playschool for her two little bunnies and other small animals. She met their mummies who told her nearly everything that went on in the countryside. Suppose a new pool had been built? Roberta would know of it. Off Betty flew to find Roberta. Slater and Benji were not long following her. They were much too excited to wait around.

HAPPIER DAYS

As Lily's friends hurried to her help, they all thought of the happy days they had had at Lily's old pool. Lily often gave parties and everyone was welcome. If they were not friendly with each other when they arrived, they soon were, and laughed, sang, played games and tucked into lovely food.

Lily's friends chuckled to themselves as they remembered her coaxing her nephew Frank, to give displays of swimming she had taught him. Frank always looked smart in the striped swimsuits she bought him, but he was so shy, he certainly needed a lot of coaxing.

ROBERTA RABBIT HAS SOMETHING TO SAY

It was at The Warrens, about half a mile from the stream that Betty found Roberta Rabbit. Roberta was talking to Tim Tortoise and Betty waggled her wings to tell the others, then she flew down. Roberta had been wheeling her bunnies back from visiting their auntie and one bit of gossip she had discovered from Auntie Rosie was just what Betty, Benji and Slater wanted to hear!

Yes, Roberta knew of a safe pool, one that had just been built by humans who had moved into the big house beyond The Warrens. What was more, she would lend Lily her pram to move all her belongings there, or what was left of them.

MOVING ON

Happily, Lily, with the pram to help her, was soon on her way to her new home. She was sure it would be very suitable and safe. Betty flew ahead to find the right path and Slater scurried behind, calling directions.

Benji and Fay Fieldmouse carried some of the things that Lily could not get into the pram.

Lily had already found she had more than one jug and more cushions than she needed. She also had two kettles. Lily felt she should do something about this.

After a while, Lily asked Fay to make two very special errands for her.

PRESENTS FOR PETER

Fay made her first errand for Lily to Peter, the very prickly hedgehog, who loved to laze in his easy chair but whose prickles soon spiked his cushions to pieces.

Lily sent Fay to him, with her biggest and strongest cushion. It was especially strong, so that her nephew Frank could sit on it on the floor, even bounce on it, without it bursting.

Lily also sent Peter a nice big milk jug. He had to fetch milk from a farm and as he drank a lot of milk, a bigger jug would certainly save him some trips. How thoughtful Lily was!

A KETTLE FULL OF MICE

Fay's next visit was to her own family, to ask them to fetch a kettle which Lily wanted them to have. They were very excited. Since the farmer had cut the corn in the field where they had lived, they now had no home for themselves. They had been staying with Auntie Fiona whose home was rather small for two families, but now Fay's family could live in the kettle. Everyone helped tow the kettle to a snug spot under a big tree and Fay left the others lining it with soft grasses. By the time she came back from helping Lily, the mice's new home would be complete.

THE WISH

At the big house by The Warrens, where Wendy and Robin's daddy had built the new pool, the two children were standing by the window, looking out into the garden.

The next day, Mummy said Wendy and Robin could go out to play. How much more fun it would be, they thought, if they had a pet to play with, but they were too young to look after a pet by themselves and Mummy was too busy with the new baby to help.

Out in the garden, Wendy gave a little cry. She had seen something move down on the pool, and off they ran to see what it was.

LILY AT HOME

There in the middle of the new pool sitting on her new pad, was Lily, smiling happily. Of course she did not wear clothes when humans were about.

The children did not go too close to the water. They had been warned that it was not safe. They clapped and laughed as Lily hopped in and out oft the water, jumping from one pad to another.

The children decided to call their new friend Lily, because she lived on the lily pond. What a coincidence Lily thought. Weren't they clever to guess her name? Lily tried to tell them, but it just sounded like a croak!

TIME FOR A PARTY

In the days that followed. Wendy and Robin found that they had more than one pet.
Lily's friends all came to bring her fresh furniture for her new home and stopped to enjoy one of her special parties.
Here Lily is having a swimming party for Frank, sister Greta and Daniel. Lily is in the middle of the pool trying to coax Frank to give a swimming display. He is still very shy.
Here we leave Lily, happily playing with her family and friends in her new home and also her new found friends Wendy and Robin, without whose new pond, Lily would not have a home.